The Poems of Lorena

Compiled and edited in loving memory by her son

The Poems of Lorena

Copyright © 2018 by Michael R. Davidson.

MRD Enterprises, Inc.

PO BOX 1000

Mount Jackson, VA 22844-1000

mrdenter@shentel.net

Library of Congress Registration Number: TXu 2-116-763

ISBN-13: 978-0-578-45195-4

Contact editor at info@michaelrdavidson.com

Cover: Photo of Lorena Nell Davidson ca. 1926

Back Cover photo of Lorena and the author 1944.

Printed and bound in the United States of America.

First printing 2019

Foreword

Publishing a compilation of my mother's poetry is something I have long contemplated. It was a labor of love, certainly, and I waited far too long to complete it. For most of her life she loved poetry, and there is no doubt she possessed a deep artistic streak. But it was not until her later years that she began to flourish.

The poetry in this book is taken from old, handwritten notes my mother kept and fortunately brought with her when she came to live with us when she was in her 90's and no longer able to live on her own. I must also thank her niece, Tricia Cramer Long, for some poems Mom left with her. Most of all, Mom loved to recite poetry and frequently regaled us and friends with her verses and tidbits of rhyming reason she'd picked up during her long and productive life.

Do not expect the grandeur of a Tennyson or the alliterative genius of a Poe. These are the words of a woman of her time, born shortly after the turn of the 20th Century. It's a sort of folk art that Mom wrote mostly for herself. Nonetheless, it is fully expressive of the composition of her character

She dearly loved her little home town of Shelburn, Indiana, and her many friends there, where she was a stalwart member of the Methodist Church. It was in that same little church that I learned about God and the redeeming virtues of Christianity which remain imprinted indelibly on my soul. Mom was deeply religious and possessed of a positive, outgoing nature, and she certainly did not fear death but looked forward to being reunited with her Savior. The depth of her religiosity is immediately evident in the poems in this little book.

And, yes, she had her prideful side, as well. The Shelburn Ruritan honored her "for her poetic contributions to the community" with a plaque naming her the town poet laureate. A few of her poems (which I have not included herein) were published by The International Library of Poetry.

Where did this remarkable woman come from? She was a small-town girl and remained one at heart her entire life. She was born Lorena Nell Cramer in Shelburn, Indiana, in 1916. Her father, Harry, was a barber, and her mother, Frances Ellen, a homemaker. Unfortunately, she and her old brother (by three years), Calvin, lost both parents very early in life. Her mother went first, a victim to the Spanish Flu that devastated so much of the country in 1918. Harry died a few years later of pneumonia. Both children went to live with their maternal grandparents, also in Shelburn.

Mom's grandmother, Mary Lucetta Sills Cramer, had a great effect on her life, and the relationship produced many stories, mostly funny, that Mom loved to tell. Grandma Cramer was a very religious woman, and she passed her deep faith on to her granddaughter.

The family was by no means well-off, but the life of young people in the 1920's was not so wrapped up in affluence as today because nobody had any money. Calvin was evidently very protective of his little sister, and Mom loved to tell how when she was in high school she would sneak out of the house to go to Sullivan, a larger town south of Shelburn, to have fun with her friends at an establishment known as the "Greasy Bear." Mom told us how she would hide under a table when Calvin came looking for her.

In her high school senior year, she was spied by a handsome young man ten years' her senior, Ernest "Zip" Davidson, who was at the time working in the auto industry in Detroit. He was a Shelburn boy who excelled at all sports and was very popular. Evidently aware of her brother's protective nature, he asked if he might ask Mom on a date. Calvin gave his blessing. After the date, Ernest told her that if she would wait for him, he would marry her someday.

She waited, and he did.

They married in 1934 and moved to Detroit. They travelled wherever Dad's work took them and finally settled in Marion, Ohio, in a duplex in a nice neighborhood. Dad had a good job at Packard. They were overjoyed when Mom became pregnant, but it ended in tragedy when the child, Richard, was stillborn, leaving them crestfallen. Finally, in 1944, I was born, but Mom could have no more children, and this was a great sorrow to her to the end of her days.

Mom and Dad's best friends in Shelburn during this period were "Check" Allison and his wife. When they were young and times were tough, they would go to a spot on the banks of the Wabash called Riverview and camp out, eating wild pawpaws and fish. Money in those days was a luxury most people learned to do without.

When World War II broke out, Dad and "Check" Allison volunteered for military service. It turned out that "Check" had flat feet, and the medics discovered that Dad had diabetes. Both were turned down for military duty. During the war Dad worked as an expert on the engine Packard was manufacturing for the P-40 fighter plane and travelled extensively in this capacity to places like Georgia and Florida.

A natural athlete, Dad was a great golfer, and one of the earliest memories I have of him is standing on a green at the Marion Country Club holding a putter while dad practiced. He was a jovial, outgoing man who made friends easily. I never heard him say a bad word about anyone – except when he was behind the wheel and expressed less than charitable opinions about other drivers. This had an unfortunate effect on me.

Taking a cue from Dad behind the wheel, one day I rode my trike up behind Mom in the kitchen and yelled, "Get out of my way, you goddammed woman driver!" I can still almost taste the soap she immediately jammed into my mouth.

I recall an incident when I was about three years old and the city had tarred the street in front of the house. Mom ordered me not to walk in the tar. But that tar was interesting, and it smelled funny. Being a clever child, I decided I would instead ride my tricycle through it. That wouldn't be disobeying, would it? When I arrived at the back door trailing three streaks of tar behind me on the sidewalk, I proudly announced, "See, I didn't walk in it." The response from Mom was immediate - a sound spanking.

But tragedy soon befell us. On the golf course, Dad noticed that his little finger was twitching, and he couldn't stop it. After an examination, the doctors told him he had Parkinson's Disease and predicted that he would be completely bedridden within a few years. This was cataclysmic news that destroyed any chance for the family to prosper. In a display of incredible callousness, Packard promptly terminated his employment.

Hard times had come, and Mom and Dad had to lower their expectations. They moved to a small Ohio town, Prospect, and Dad got a job selling Allis Chalmers farm equipment, which required him to spend a lot of time on the road. Nevertheless, he never failed to take me to the movies for a western double feature every Saturday. Dad loved westerns, and his favorite author was Zane Grey.

Finally, even that job petered out, and my parents moved back to Shelburn where Dad's older brother, Herb, was a foreman at the Dresser Coal Mine. Dad and Herb had worked in the mines when they were teenagers to support their family after their father died. Herb got Dad a job as an electrician in the mine.

We moved into an apartment in a house owned by a blind lady, "Charlie" Crosby, who lived downstairs with her Pekinese dog. It wasn't much, but Dad was making ends meet. Finally, in 1949, they managed to buy a house on Broad Street in Shelburn, but in May of that same year, not long after my fifth birthday, a severe tornado destroyed half the town and killed many people.

I remember the day well. The sky turned a venomous shade of green and hail began to fall. Out in the yard, I had fun collecting the golf ball size hail stones. A short while later we were in the kitchen when there was a roar. Dad commented that it must be a train, but Mom said, "If it's a train, it's coming down the street outside." Dad looked out the back window and saw houses and debris filling the air. At that moment, our house was struck. The vacuum sucked out the window glass and lifted me right off the kitchen floor and started to pull me out of a window, but Dad grabbed me and huddled against an inner wall behind the sewing machine.

Mom had other concerns. She'd only the day before hung new curtains, and when the windows blew out, the curtains were being sucked outside. She was determined to save them. Every time she ran past us, Dad tried to grab her, but she eluded his grasp. She looked up just in time to see our washing machine, an imposing appliance, flying through the house directly toward her. This convinced her to join us against the wall. At that moment, the storm lifted the house off its foundation. Dad said, "Hold on. We're going for an airplane ride," undoubtedly trying to reassure me. Fortunately, the storm then settled the house back down. When it was over, we made our way across town to my Grandmother's house. The west side of town had not been harmed, at all.

I was deathly afraid of storms for years afterwards and trembled at the sound of thunder.

Mom and Dad found another house at the edge of town, and we settled there. That house remained home for decades until we moved Mom into an assisted living facility.

Times were tough. Dad secured a position as an accountant at Allis Chalmers in Terre Haute, but money was tight, and his Parkinsons was not getting any better. To make ends meet, Mom took a low-paying job at a small packaging plant in Shelburn.

Throughout all the hardship suffered by Mom and Dad, I never had any idea that we were poor. Growing up in that small, rural town gifted me with a Huckleberry Finn childhood with fishing and long bike rides with friends out into the countryside. Mom and Dad made sure I never wanted for anything, and it was only as I grew older that I realized how tough things were for them.

I remember long Summer days fishing with Dad out at the old Glendora Mine pond. Mom always made sure Christmas was special. My parents never exchanged gifts, making sure I received everything on my Christmas list.

At last, Dad's Parkinsons affected him so much he could not work. In 1957 he underwent experimental brain surgery in Indianapolis. The surgery required him to remain conscious as the surgeons drilled through his skull and inserted a long needle into his brain. Pure alcohol was injected to kill the nerve center that controlled the disease. Parkinsonians do not shake when they sleep, and Dad had to be conscious to determine the effect of the surgery. The procedure was partially successful in stopping the shaking on one side of his body, but Dad adamantly refused to go through another such harrowing procedure to correct the other side. In the late-1950's he was awarded full disability by the Social Security Administration and began receiving Black Lung benefits from his time in the coal mines. Mom found a good job as a laboratory technician at the Pfizer plant near Terre Haute. Later she found work with the Reuben H. Donnelly Corporation as a proofreader.

In the meantime, I married, spent four years in the Army and had a son, a grandchild Mom and Dad doted over. Following the Army, I was recruited by the Central Intelligence Agency, and for the next 28 years spent most of the time in various countries abroad or in Washington. We were living in Paris in 1985 when we received news that my Dad had passed away.

Dad's passing left Mom completely independent. It had not been easy working full time and helping Dad as his illness progressed. As time passed, she became heavily involved in community affairs, especially in the Methodist Church. She was also administrator of the local Community Center. Her circle of friends grew, and she thrived. She was elected Senior Queen of Sullivan County and in 1995 was the Shelburn Ruritan's Citizen of the Year.

She continued her lifelong practice of jotting down bits of folk wisdom and poetry she read and liked and composed her own verses. She dabbled in oil painting, as well, and some of her paintings hang still today in friends' homes. Her poems were published in several collections and were well-known throughout Sullivan County. In recognition of her poetic contributions to the community the Shelburn Ruritan named her Poet Laureate. She continued to write and recite poetry to the end of her days.

For many years, she maintained a small apartment in the Shelburn assisted living facility and took great pride in it and in her independence. Always a good cook, she enjoyed baking pies for charity events.

But most of all, she loved her friends and her little town. Shelburn was by this time well down on its heels. The mines had petered out decades earlier, and the population was only around 1,000. Well into her nineties, Mom was still driving her big Chevrolet, shopping, meeting with friends, and writing.

When at last she could no longer be left on her own, she came to live with us in Virginia, but she regretted it almost from the day she arrived. She wanted to be in Shelburn, and she pined for her town every day.

She rests there today in Little Flock Cemetery beside Dad. They've become part of the soil of the Shelburn they loved and will be there forever.

Michael R. Davidson
June 2018, New Market, VA

The Poems of Lorena

Edited in loving memory by her son

Definition of a Christian

A Christian is a person whose thoughts and actions are conditioned by the spirit and teachings of Christ. He is thoroughly dedicated as a disciple and sincerely endeavors to live as Christ lived. A Christian is one who has experienced a spiritual transformation of mind and soul.

Lorena N. Davidson

TODAY – TOMORROW –ALWAYS

God bless you with His love,
And in His goodness shower you
With graces from above.
May He be part of all you do
And hear your ev'ry prayer
Today – tomorrow –always
God keep you in his care.

I'M THANKFUL FOR THE LITTLE THINGS

I'm thankful for the little things
God gives along the way,
The sun that shines the birds that sing,
The strength to face each day.
I'm thankful for the home I share
With a family filled with love,
And for the voice that says – I care
From our Father up above.
But I'm thankful most of all
Just to be a child of His,
For no matter how deep or far I fall,
I know that he forgives.

SAID THE ROBIN TO THE SPARROW

Said the robin to the sparrow,
I should really like to know
Why those anxious human beings
Rush about and worry so.
Said the sparrow to the robin,
Well, I think that it must be
That they have no heavenly Father
Such as cares for you and me.

IF GOD CARES FOR UNCLEAN BIRDS

If God cares for unclean birds,
How much does he care for redeemed saints
who will inhabit Heaven?

DO NOT LOOK FORWARD

Do not look forward to what might happen tomorrow;
The same Everlasting Father who cares for you today
Will take care of your tomorrow and every day.
Either He will shield you from suffering
Or He will give you the unfailing strength to bear it.
Be at peace, then, and put aside
All anxious thoughts and imaginations.

YOU SAY THE WORLD LOOKS GLOOMY

You say the world looks gloomy,
The skies are grim and gray;
The night has lost its quiet;
You fear the coming day.
Each morn is like a rosebud
Just waiting to unfold.
You can turn the night to day,
And make the moments gold.
The world is what you make it;
The sky is gray or blue,
Just as your soul may paint it;
It's not the world – it's you.

BLESSINGS

These are the blessings
I wish for you:
Health and happiness
All your life through,
The pleasure of doing
The work you like best,
Hours of leisure
For play and for rest,
Pride in the things
You've accomplished so far,
Wisdom to know
What your goals really are,

Patience when problems
Arrive at your door,
Belief that still
Happier years are in store,
The blessing of friends
Who will make your days bright,
A strong sense of humor
To keep your heart light,
And always the knowledge
That God up above
Is caring for you
With his infinite love.

I'M GLAD

I'm glad the Great Creator
Arranged for there to be
A bit of work left over
For the likes of you and me.

I'm sure He could have finished things,
For instance, made the bread.
But no, He chose to give us little
Grains of wheat instead.

I'm sure he could have planted houses
With no strain or fuss,
Instead He planted trees and left
The building up to us.

I think He wanted us to share
That joy and sheer elation
That builders and creators know
Who see their own creation.

THE THINGS YOU CANNOT BUY

The best and sweetest things in life
Are things you cannot buy.
The music of the birds at dawn,
The rainbow in the sky,
The dazzling magic of the stars,
The miracle of light,
The precious gifts of health and strength,
Of hearing, speech and sight,
The peace of mind that crowds
A busy life of work well done,
A faith in God that deepens
As you face the setting sun,
The bloom of love, the joy of friendship,
As the years go by.
You find the greatest blessings
Are the things you cannot buy.

IF

If –
God can hang the stars on high,
Can paint the clouds we see drift by,
Can send the sun across the sky,
What could He do through you?

If –
He can send a storm through space,
And dot with trees the mountain's face;
If He the sparrow's way can trace,
What could He do through you?

If –
God can do such little things
As count our hairs, make birds that sing,
Control the universe that swings,
What could he do for you?

EVERY TIME I PASS A CHURCH

Every time I pass a church,
I go in for a little visit,
So, when comes the day I'm carried in,
The Lord won't ask, "Who is it?"

WHEN YOU GET TO HEAVEN

When you get to Heaven,
And look around to see who's there,
Don't be surprised, try not to stare,
For doubtless there will many be,
Who'll wonder what you're doing there.

IN GAPS BETWEEN OUR WORK AND PLAY

In gaps between our work and play
We're often "killing time," we say;
But it was never really thus,
For time, instead, is killing us.

GOD HATH NOT PROMISED

God hath not promised
Skies always blue,
Flower-strewn pathways
All our lifetimes through;
God hath not promised
Sun without rain,
Joy without sorrow,
Peace without pain.

But God hath promised
Strength for the day,
Rest from the labor,
Light for the way,
Help from above,
Grace for the trials,
Unfailing sympathy,
Undying love.

OLD AGE AND RETIREMENT[1]

I'm sixty-two years old today,
And strange as it may seem,
I don't worry about the hair of gray
Or things that might have been.

My legs are weak, my hearing's bad,
My body's overweight,
But worse things than this I've had,
So, I'd say that I feel great.

I'm looking forward this next year
To a free and easy life,
Content and happy and full of cheer,
Away from toil and strife.

So, don't worry about this old Nell,
Or wonder about my fate.
The alarm will never ring its bell
And for work I won't be late.

---

[1] Published in Reuben H. Donnelly magazine (1978).

Instead I'll rock and sleep and rest
In my big rocking chair
And know this life is the very best
And to avoid it, I wouldn't dare.

I'll be content as a sitting hen,
And free as a running deer.
Life will be much sweeter then,
When I retire from here.

So, let me tell you this, my friends,
If you're sorry as you can be,
Old age to me is not the end,
But the beginning of life for me.

✳✳✳✳✳

OUR VOLUNTEERS

A volunteer is someone
Whose heart is feeling right.
They'll work 'til day is done
And far into the night.

They don't expect a back-slap,
Nor pay for what they do.
One smiling face or hand-clasp
Will more than see them through.

They're always there to aid you
When others turn away,
Thinking not of payment due,
But to brighten up the day.

From the ones who drive the wheels,
Or call to chat a while,
To the ones who take the meals,
We salute you with a smile.

LOVE

All we need is a little love
To brighten up our day.
It comes from our dear God above
And will show to us the way.

So, love the people of every race.
That's all you have to do.
The world will be a better place,
And God's love will shine on you.

DO YOU FALL APART

Do you fall apart
when the going gets tough?
Are you lost in a sea of despair?
Do you feel that the road's become too rough?
Do you think nobody cares?
Just put your faith in the Lord up above.
With Him all your burdens share.
He will fill you up with peace and love,
When you go to Him in prayer.

REST[2]

Many people prize earthly things,
Cars, houses, big diamond rings,
Their thoughts are on what they can do
To get more money for something new.

How foolish these humans here on earth;
They toil almost from the day of their birth,
To store up treasures and pile them high,
To leave behind the day they die.

How different all their lives would be
If they'd only open their eyes and see
That earthly goods cannot them save
When at last they're put into the grave.

It's not the earthly treasures that count,
Nor the money we leave in any account,
But the treasure that's stored within the heart,
When at last this earth we do depart.

So, love your neighbors and love your friend,
And never on earthly things depend,
But put your faith in God above,
Trust in His unbounded love.

Then when you take that final walk
And meet your Maker and have a talk,
You'll find that yours was the life spent best,
With love and peace, you'll find your rest.

---

[2] Published in Alumni Newsletter, March 1983. Received honorable mention, "New World of Poetry Contest," December 1983

PRAYER

Why is this day so full of gloom,
With storm clouds in the sky?
Why am I hidden in my room?
Why do I want to cry?

Perhaps I wouldn't feel so beat
If I'd only think to pray,
And lay my cares a Jesus' feet.
Then the sun would shine today.

All it takes is a gentle plea,
And God's help is on the way.
So, pray that everyone may see
What brightens up our day.

OUR SON

We've been together for years, you see.
We've weathered the storms of life.
We've managed to keep our sanity
Through all the toil and strife.

Our marriage was blessed with one son,
Although we wanted more.
We figured God's will be done,
So, started on the chore

Of raising up first one child,
To teach him right from wrong.
We didn't want him to be wild,
But to start each day with song.

To us our son has been a joy
Far more than any riches.
He grew up as a normal boy,
Just keeping us in stitches.

We tried to teach him of God above
And the beauty all about
And to depend upon His love
And never ever doubt

That God would keep him throughout life
And care for his ev'ry need,
So he could weather the toil and strife
And pass the faith to his own seed.

Se We'll leave this legacy to our boy
And hope that he will raise
That grandson up to be a joy,
Giving God the praise.

*****

MOTHER

What is a mother?
It's plain to see
She's like no other
In the family.

She'll give you're a smack
When you do wrong
Then pick you up
And sing you a song.

She'll threaten, cajole you,
And fill you with fear
Of punishment you're due,
Then call you dear.

She'll be your nurse
When you are sick
And empty her purse
To cure you quick.

She'll loan you the car
To go out on a date
Then say – Don't go far
And please don't be late.

She'll say you can swim
Just don't get wet.
She'll cater to your whim,
Then make you forget

What you wanted before.
So, give her your love,
And don't think it a chore,
And thank God above

For a mother who cares
All her life through
And a mother who shares
All God's love with you.

*****

GRANDMA

God answers prayer; this I was taught
As I stood at my Grandmother's knee.
Her Bible gave me food for thought
And opened a new world to me.

She tried to teach me right from wrong,
And I didn't always obey,
But she would end each day with a song
And thank God for another day.

Her memory lives on in my heart,
And now that I've older grown,
I thank God for that Christian start
And for the love to me that was shown.

I try now to end the day with a prayer,
But I still don't always obey.
I know she watches from that Golden Stair,
Still thanking God for the day.

Someday I hope to meet her there
On that Golden Stair, you see.
Then we can both kneel in prayer
And praise God through eternity.

THIS PEACE HE GIVES

I know not why my pathway leads through
Valleys rough and steep;
But this I know, while walking there,
I've found communion sweet,

With those I love, and, best of all,
With Him who climbed for me,
Beneath the heavy cross, the hill,
That led to Calvary.

I know not why so many props
Have gently been removed,
But I know through every loss
His arms unfailing proved.

I have no reason – none at all
To doubt His precious Word,
Though all I love be swept away,
His voice would still be heard

Above the storm, and as I lift
My tear-filled eyes to him;
The Great Creator, Lord of all,
He whispers "Peace" within.

So, as I look beyond today,
I pray that I may share,
This peace he gives to those who have
A greater cross to bear.

I know not how long 'twill be before
He calls me home,
But this I know – beneath His wings,
I'll never be alone.

*****

MY GRANDSON

I thought I'd never have such joy
As on the day I held my boy,
But then that grandson came along
And filled my heart with love and song.
His eyes so blue – his hair so blond.
It was as if he held a wand
To captivate and hold my heart,
The love and pleasure to impart.
Today that lad has grown so tall,
I wait and listen for his call
To tell me things are going right.
I know he's happy on this night
Because his wife's so sweet and dear,
Is always by his side so near.
Perhaps someday a child will come,
Bright and beautiful as the sun
To fill their days with pride and joy,
Perhaps another bouncing boy.
But if I never live to see
Another child so dear to me,
Then let me say with all my heart,
I would not from my mem'ries part,
In sending me my family,
So, I sing praise to God above
For endowing me with all this love.

NAMES

What's in a name?
It's plain to see
I could not be a James,
Nor even a Henry.
From the very beginning
It's been ever so
That a girl must be a Jenny,
And a boy must be a Joe.
Some folks change it
And call a girl Jim.
But why rearrange it
So, we'll think a girl's a him?
So, when baby is born
And announcements are due
We won't feel forlorn
If the name gives a clue
Whether girl or boy
Who's arrived this day.
It will be a joy,
That's all I can say.
We'll know what to buy,
Whether pink or blue.
So, on this rely,
And don't name him Sue.

EASTER[3]

On this earth a long time ago, Christ walked
In the midst of men.
And the people ridiculed and mocked,
For prejudice existed even then.

He was looked upon with scorn,
Oh, how He must have paid
From the day when He was born
Till the day He was betrayed.

He carried the cross up the hill,
And there was crucified.
And the prophecy was fulfilled
When on that cross he died.

He suffered much when he was nailed,
Of this I'm very sure.
When on the cross he was impaled,
Such pain he did endure.

---

[3] Written for her church's Easter service in 1983

They took him down from that old cross
And placed him in the tomb
While Mother Mary mourned the loss
Of the issue of her womb.

But three days later Christ arose,
Triumphant from the grave,
He was the one His Father chose
All men on earth to save.

He was caught up into the sky,
How wonderful it must have been
To see the clouds His death belie
And know he lived again.

So, Easter is a glorious day.
It's a day for you and me
And to the world we all proclaim,
He died for humanity.

So, live your life the way he would.
Fill your heart with grace and love.
Do the things you know you should,
And someday dwell with Him above.

*****

MOTHER

God thought to give the sweetest thing
In His almighty power, and deeply pondering
What it should be – one hour,
In fondest joy and love or heart
Outweighing every other
He moved the gates of Heaven apart
And gave the earth a mother.

*

MOTHER AND GOD

A partnership with God is motherhood.
What strength, what purity, what self-control,
What love, what wisdom should belong to her
Who helps God fashion an immortal soul.

MEMORIES[4]

In my back yard there stands a tree.
It's old and bent and bare.
Remembering things that used to be
A swing I can envision there
Where once a little boy did play,
And childhood laughter filled the air
With happiness beyond compare.
My yard is empty now of sound.
That boy is all full grown
And on his life's career is bound
With a small lad of his own.
Someday the memories will be his
As mine belong to me,
And he will always think of this
Each time he sees that tree.
So, store your mem'ries in your heart
And never let them go.
Then they will in another start,
For this one thing I know.
Memories are passed from son to son,
May ever be it so,
And when you have life's battle won,
Those memories still will grow.

---

[4] Published in Alumni Newsletter, October 1983; "World of Poetry" Silver Pact Award. Honored with a Golden Poet Award by the National Library of Poetry. Dedicated to son, Michael.

BLUE BOY, THE STRAY CAT

He came to me bedraggled and all wet,
So very lank and lean.
I tried hard to ignore him, and yet
I wondered where he might have been.
His skinny legs, his long, thin tail,
How ugly he seemed to be.

But at my back door without fail
He would daily come to see
If there was a bit of meat
Or perhaps a saucer of milk.
And he would roll about my feet,
And rub my leg, fur as soft as silk.

So, at last I took him in
To feed and pet and guard,
It seemed to me some kind of sin
To chase him from my yard.
He showed me he was not a fool
When he promptly found that place
Where he could perch upon a stool,
The relief showed in his face.

Later in the day I found
That the stool was unoccupied
And Blue Boy cat was toilet bound,
When the bathtub drain he spied.
Into the tub he leapt,
And over the drain did perch
And there his appointment kept.
Not to be left in the lurch.

For all the beauty he might lack
He makes up with love and pride,
So, I would never put him back
Into the world outside.
So, to the animals please be kind
When they come to find a home,
And maybe you will find
A Blue Boy of your own.

*****

THE PROMISE

The sky is blue, the grass is green.
There's color all about.
No lovelier things than these I've seen.
Of this I have no doubt.
God made the wonderful universe
For people to enjoy.
He set the stars and moon traverse
To be the sky's convoy.
He made the sun to warm the day,
The clouds to bring the rain.
He created man from out the clay,
And gave to him a brain
With which to think and do his work
And ever to believe
If his duties he did not shirk,
A reward he would receive
Of a heavenly home on high
More beautiful than this earth.
On this he could rely
From the moment of his birth.
This is the promise to all mankind,
To dwell with God one day.
So, use your body and your mind
In a faithful Christian way.

MY INDIANA HOME

The years I've spent in Indiana
Are the best years of my life.
I've managed to be happy
Amid the toil and strife.

I've lived in several other States
When I was bent to roam,
But came back to the place that rates,
My sweet Indiana home.

The winters are so very cold,
The summer air is hot,
But balmy days slip in between,
So, the bad ones are forgot.

When I gaze upon the sky
And see that vast expanse
Of billowing clouds and sun by day,
At night the stars that dance,

It's then that I thank God
For this mighty universe,
The sun, the moon, the stars above
Which o'er the earth traverse.

I thank Him for my eyes that see
This beauty all around
And for the life He gave to me
In this, the greatest State.

So, let's be happy with our home,
Sing its praises long and loud,
And for the things we have on earth
Be thankful and so proud.

God meant us to enjoy it all,
The things He did create.
So, lift your voices high and clear
For our Indiana State.

*****

THE TIME

Why do I wonder? Why do I weep?
Why do I ponder, unable to sleep?
What's on my mind? What can it be?
Why can't I find what's bothering me?

Why didn't I pray before going to bed?
Why didn't I say, "By Him I'll be led?"
Why not ask God, then, to help me some way,
To forgive me my sins of this past day?

So, drop to your knees each night of your life,
Ask God to ease the trial and the strife.
He'll answer your prayer if you only obey,
And lighten your care, just take time to pray.

A GIFT

Each morn is like a rosebud
Just waiting to unfold.
You can turn the night to day
And make the moments gold.

Each day is what you make it.
The skies are gray or blue.
God gives the day to use;
The rest is up to you.

So, make the most of all your time,
Use it well and learn
Each day is a gift from God
Which never can return.

ROSES AND BEES

We stopped to smell the roses
Like the song told us to do,
But the bees lit on our roses,
And that made us very blue.

The bees sat down a bit too hard,
Of that we have no doubt,
So, don't listen to that bard
When he begins to shout.

Stop and smell those roses
You find along the way,
For the pain that's in your noses
Will last longer than the day.

GET RIGHT WITH GOD

Where are you going, my dear friend?
What are you searching for?
Are you on a path without an end?
Or in a room without a door?

Are your feelings all pent up inside?
Do you think there's no one to care?
Someone heard you when you cried
And wants all y our burdens to share.

So, open your mind and heart to God.
Your troubles will all disappear.
He'll answer your prayer with a smiling nod
And fill your soul with cheer.

The right path will soon be found,
Locked doors will open wide,
And your spirit will upward bound
With our dear God by your side.

THE SHRINE

In my heart there is a Shrine,
A place for God to stay.
It holds all His love, oh, so divine
And brightens up each day.
I can talk to Him at any time
When shadows 'round me fall,
When life has no sense nor rhyme
And seems worth naught, at all,
His voice comes to me sweet and clear
Whispering, "Peace, be still."
It dulls the pain and all the fear.
When I answer to His will
The days take on a brighter glow
And shadows behind me fall.
It brings my spirit up from low
And the pain I don't recall.

GOD'S LOVE

There never was a day so dark
That God's love shining through
Could fail to scatter every cloud
And turn the skies to blue.

There never was a road so rough
To rugged or so long
That God's inspiring presence
Couldn't give the heart a song.

There never was a burden
That His strong arms can't bear.
There never was a problem
Impossible with prayer.

OUR TOWN THEN AND NOW

Today the town's a different place.
Some things have quickly been erased
And others gone down like the sun.
Time takes its toll on everyone.

The prices are high, the cars are fast.
My life's a blend of present and past.
But through it all I'm here to say
I wouldn't have it another way.

Just take the changes and be calm.
Remember the washboard and outside john.
Forget the then – remember the now,
And let old Shelburn take a bow.

OUR SENIOR CENTER

In this town there is a place,
A haven for the old
Where you see a wrinkled face,
But hearts are young and bold.

Father Time may wash away
The beauty and the grace,
As with each passing day
Our lives we have to face.

Age is just a state of mind.
We seniors know full well.
But when we are in a bind
Here's one thing that I'll tell:

The Center helps us all to ease
The loneliness and pain
As we try our best to please
Happiness is our gain.

Someone to say, "How are you?"
And greet you with a smile.
Someone to sit beside you
And chat a little while.

So, lunch is a time to talk.
It comes each day at noon.
Wednesday is the day to walk
To keep our hearts in tune.

Our policy an open door
To those who wish to come.
With arts, crafts and games galore
There's fun for everyone.

When Father Time tolls the bell,
And my lifespan is o'er,
Someone will be there still
To greet you at the door.

So, I thank God for this place
Where fellowship prevails,
And hope to contain the pace
'Til my last ship sets sail.

*****

HAIR RAISING EPISODE[5]

These two old ladies lived in town.
One was Smith, the other Brown.
To name real names would be a sin,
So fictitious names we use herein.
Into a restaurant they stopped to dine,
Had fish and fries but eschewed the wine.
They finished the meal, got up to leave
When on the chair Smith stubbed a toe.
The toe caught on that old chair.
She fell on the floor and lost her hair.
That wig flew off with a bound
While laughing loudly was Lady Brown.
Smith went scrambling for her wig
With Lady Brown still laughing big.
A man came over trying to help,
But Smith got up by herself.
He said, "I wonder what got you drunk."
Smith answered, "That water really packed a punch."
Out of the restaurant Smith and Brown did go
Thinking they'd put on quite a show.
The diners laughed as they opened the door.
I think they thought there might be more.
"Enough is enough," said Lady Brown,
"Let's see if we can get back to town."

[5] A true story of how Lorena lost her wig after having lunch with a friend.

MY PRAYER FOR YOU

I said a prayer for you today
And know God must have heard.
I felt the answer in my heart
Although He spoke no word.

I didn't ask for wealth or fame.
I know you wouldn't mind.
I for a diff'rent treasure
Of a more lasting kind.

I asked that He'd be near you
At the start of every day
To grant you health and blessings
And friends to share your way.

I asked for happiness for you
In all things great and small.
But it was for His loving care
I prayed for most of all.

HOME FOR THE EVENING CHRISTMAS EVE[6]

The lights in the windows are gleaming.
The fire is warming my feet.
I sit in my chair just dreaming.
This time of year is so sweet.

The aroma of cookies baking,
The sweetness boggles my mind.
I could from the kitchen be taking
Choice bits of most every kind.

The ground and the trees covered with snow,
Oh, what a beautiful sight.
The houses stand all in a row
Just waiting for Christmas Eve night.

The smoke from the chimney touches the sky
And swirls in the falling snow.
The jingle of a sleigh passing by,
And the voices of people I know.

---

[6] A friend sent Lorena a Christmas card and asked her to write a poem about it.

Children all snuggled in their beds
Will soon hear the bells on the sleigh,
Awakening their sleepy heads
Knowing Santa is on his way.

The hustle and bustle of Christmas Morn,
The families coming to call
From oldest to the newly born
They each are a part of it all.

Remember that Christmas morn
So many long years ago
When unto us a Child was born
As pure as the driven snow.

So, bow your heads and thank God above
For all the things He has done,
Filling our hearts with peace and with love
By sending his only Son.

*****

IF EVERY DAY WERE CHRISTMAS

If every day were Christmas
How different life would be.
If not one day, but all the year
Was filled with charity.
Had we the faith in miracles,
A child has Christmas morn,
Then every day would be love's manger,
And Christ would be reborn
In us again to mend and still our anger,
Useless wars and ways.
Had we a child's or shepherd's gift
For wonderment and praise.
Yet every day is Christmas
When Love's law we all obey,
Not how to get but how to give,
And like a child can pray,
And like a child can wonder,
But have the grown-up vision
To give ourselves away.

TRICIA ELLEN
(To Tricia from Aunt Nell)

I once knew a baby called Trish.
She was such a sweet little dish
Who grew up way too fast,
Good things just don't last.

So, we had to get used to our girl
Who turned out to be quite a pearl.
She taught the kids at school,
Showing them to mind the rule.

But even that didn't last.
Now it's all in the past.
Today she has a different life
Learning to be a good wife.

Next step came the baby boy
Who brought them so much joy,
So that made her a mother,
And then came another.
Two boys are quite a lot to raise.

Her husband is quite a man,
Helping her with every plan.
Someday those boys will be full-grown,
And have families of their own.

Then grandpa and grandma can sit back
And rest their bodies in the sack,
But wait a minute before you go,
Let the rest go real slow.

Remember that grandkids come along
To fill their hearts with another song.
To end this story, I cannot say
But you'll know it all some fine day.

*****

GRANDMA'S GINGHAM APRON

My grandma's gingham apron
Was not for style or show.
There were no special patterns
With bright designs aglow.

She chose the apron gingham
Of checked brown and blue or gray
And "made it up in no time,"
I often heard her say.

There were no nice fancy curves,
No ruffles to arrange,
No appliques to fasten,
No rick-rack for the change.

It was gathered at the belt
That tied so neat behind,
And hemmed in at the bottom,
As straight as you could find.

There was the little pocket,
Remembered all my years;
That's where she kept the kerchief
To wipe my childhood tears.

My grandma looked so lovely
In those days so long since gone
As she stood there in the doorway
With her gingham apron on.

GRANDMA'S BONNET

My grandma wore a bonnet,
Starched stiff as it could be,
With frills and ruffles on it
For all the world to see.

She made it all of calico
With colors bright and gay.
Under her chin she tied a bow
And wore it every day.

Brown eyes twinkled 'neath the brim,
A smile upon her face,
With that bow against her chin,
The ruffles all in place.

In my dreams I see her still
Standing by the door
Wearing that bonnet with a frill
In happy days of yore.

God called her home on high
To reap her just reward
In that heaven in the sky
To dwell there with the Lord.

Does my grandma have a bonnet
In heaven's land to wear,
With frills and ruffles on it
Standing by the Golden Stair?

THE TOUCH OF GOD

Many things touch our lives each day,
A friendly smile, a child at play,
A gay hello from a passing man,
The knowledge we've done all we can
To make this world a better place,
To live and really earn our space.
Green shoots coming from the ground,
The endless blessings that abound,
The sweetness of a loving heart
That pleasures to us all impart,
Flowers that bloom in the spring,
Ears to hear the church bells ring.
All these things are but a few
That touch the lives of me and you.
So, each day surely there must be
The touch of God in all we see.

COMING HOME

There's never been a home so dear
As Shelburn, the place I call home.
Whenever I traveled far or near
It seemed I was alone.
I ached to see my old pals
And talk to them a while.
I loved to chat with those old gals
And see their happy smiles.
I'm glad to be home again
And hope that I can stay.
I even like to hear the train
That comes through town each day.
So, if it be God's will
To let me live another year,
I'll be right here still
In this place I hold so dear.

BACK HOME IN INDIANA

Back home in Indiana
Is the place I long to be.
There's no question about it.
It satisfies me.

I love my friends and neighbors, too,
And all the folks around
The old ones and the new ones
The best that I have found.

You can look the whole world over
And never find a one.
You never will discover
A substitute for some.

I love my family – Oh – as much
I like to be with them.
I want to always keep in touch
Whether talking or by pen.

They've offered their home to me
And that is good to hear
So many now forget the ones
That they should hold most dear.

No one can ever take the place
Of my son or daughter true.
They are the pride of my life,
And they still have lots to do.

All will be well,
God has it in his plan.
They have a story yet to tell
And will pass the last exam.

Their lives are yet to live
And mine is almost gone.
So, make us happy down the road
And leave us with a song.

Back home in Indiana
Is the place I long to be.
There's no question about it.
It satisfies me.

✽✽✽✽✽

MARCH 11, 2008

I was ninety-two yesterday,
And strange as it may seem,
I don't worry about this hair of gray
Or things that might have been.
My gait is slow, my hearing's bad,
I've lost a lot of weight.
But worse things than this I've had,
So, despite it all, I still feel great.
I may be here again next year
To greet you all with love.
But if I'm gone,
Don't shed a tear.
I hope to be with God above.

NO ONE EXPECTED ME

I dreamed God came the other night
And Heaven's gate swung wide.
With kindly grace an angel
Welcomed me inside.
And there to my astonishment
Stood folks I'd known on earth.
Some I had judged and labeled
As unfit with little worth.
Then angry words rose to my lips
But never were set free.
For every face showed stunned surprise.
No one expected me.

The Poems of Lorena

Memories

The Poems of Lorena

A poem Lorena learned from her grandmother.
Attribution unknown.[7]

I'm only a stone in the building
And one of the smallest there.
But the Builder had need of such a one
As He raised the temple fair.
The climbing vines may hide me,
And the shadows across me fall,
But One there is who expects me to stay
Firm in the massive wall.
Within are gifted voices caught by the passing breeze,
And fingers thrilled with His mighty love
Are touching the organ keys.
But all through the splendid music
The Builder thinks of me,
A little gray stone in the outer wall
Placed where he wants me to be.

---

[7] Lorena's note about this poem: This "... is a poem my grandmother Cramer recited to me when I was just a little girl. I think that she composed it. She was interested in poetry and read a lot of it."

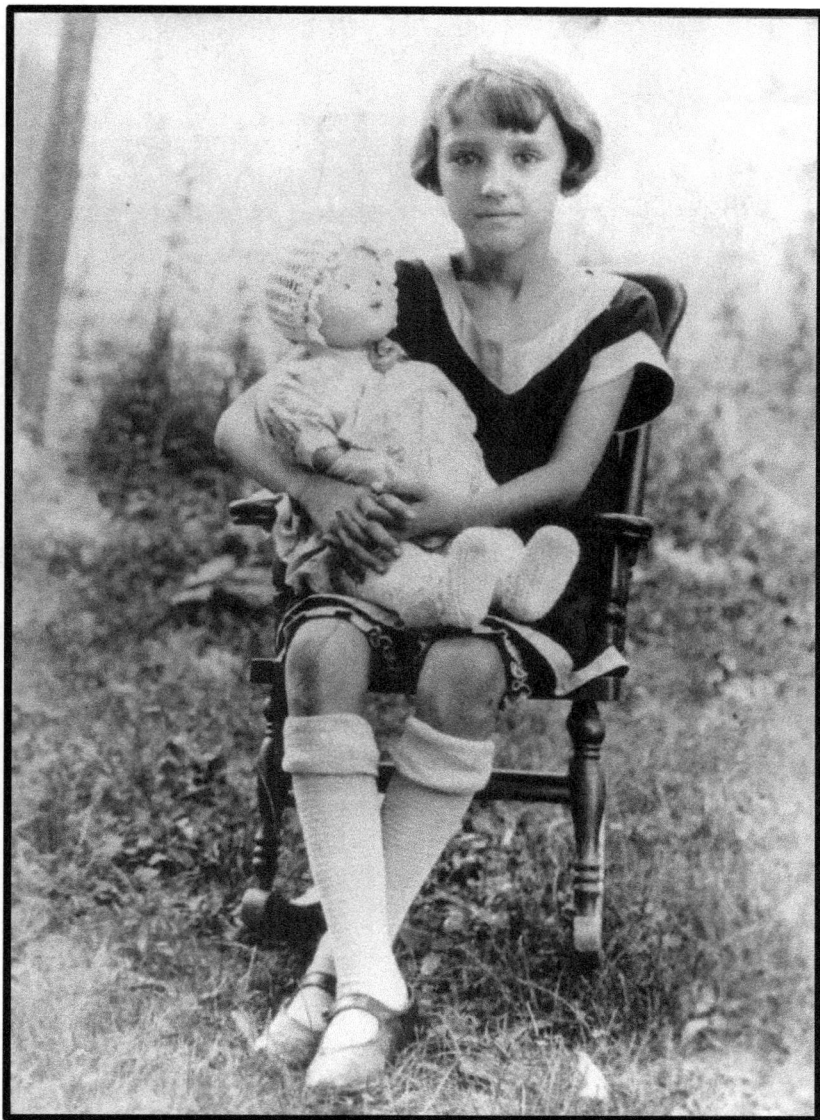

Lorena Nell Cramer with her favorite doll.
About 10 years old.

Lorena's parents, Harry and Frances Ellen Cramer

The orphans:
Lorena at 3 years old in 1919
with her older brother, 6 years old,
Calvin.

Ellen (Lorena's mother) with school class. She's third from
the right in the front row

Lorena and Calvin with their dog

High School

High School

Mom to be – Ca 1943

Mom and friend with soft drinks in front of a bait shop, probably at Riverview

Proud mother – May 1944

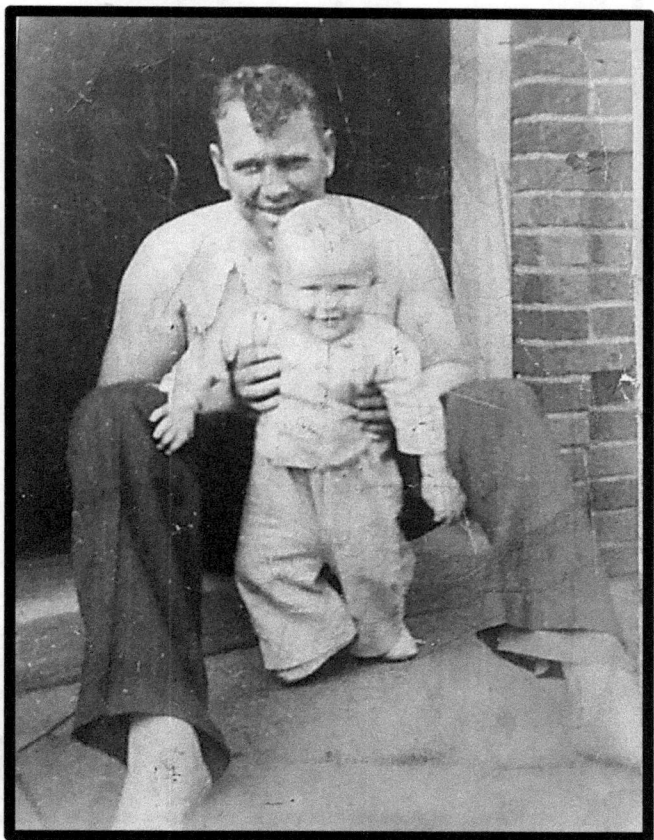

Proud husband and father – ca. 1945

Ca. 1960

2009

The Poems of Lorena

Works of fiction
by
Michael R. Davidson
www.michaelrdavidson.com

Harry's Rules
Incubus
The Incubus Vendetta
Eye for an Eye
The Inquisitor and the Maiden
Retribution
Krystal
The Dove
The Dead Lawyer
Buy Another Day

The Poems of Lorena